Coming Home to

WISWELL

LINDA FAY CLARK

Coming Home to Wiswell

Linda Fay Clark

ISBN (Print Edition): 978-1-54395-141-7

ISBN (eBook Edition): 978-1-54395-142-4

DEDICATION

To my sisters, who lived many of these memories with me.
Iva Nel, age 93, who spent her life caring for others, and is now in a Nursing Center, and dependent on family, friends, and staff, for her own care.
Rebecca, who is in Heaven, laughing at these memories, with the rest of the Angels.

CHAPTER 1: AN ORDINARY SUNDAY

———◆———

It seemed like an ordinary Sunday morning at the Wilkerson's house. We heard the church bells ring out, and we knew we had just enough time to get to church in time for Sunday School. Immediately following the sound of the bells, we heard an impatient blast of the car horn by Papa, who was already in the car ready to go. Never mind that Mama had herself and the five children to dress and get ready.

Usually on Sundays, Mama got up earlier than the rest of the family, and cooked a full meal to be ready to eat when we got home. The church goers were all friends and neighbors, and a casual invitation to "go home with us for dinner", (which is what we called the noon meal) just might be accepted by another family, and there would always be enough food.

My Aunt Virginia, Uncle William and their children Harry and Mary Beth usually came to our house for Sunday dinner every week. Though William vowed he did not like chicken, nor any fowl, he did condescend to eat the big (or so it looked to us kids!) juicy pulley bone portion, while the children looked on in envy. When finished he would allow two of us to have the bone to pull apart while making a wish; perhaps we were wishing to get to eat the pulley bone piece next time! Mama also fried the chicken gizzard for William, and he was welcome to it!

But today was different. After church we were going to Aunt Virginia's house for her birthday dinner. Since we lived on a farm, it was a treat to visit Aunt Virginia's family, who lived in town, and who had many conveniences inherent with city living. For example, warm central heat versus our chilly house heated only with a fireplace; running water, while we had to draw water from the well; paved streets and sidewalks that were ideal for roller skating, unlike our gravel road. Of course we had no roller skates anyway.

On this particular Sunday afternoon, December 7, 1941, the grown ups were in a somber mood. After dinner they were listening intently to the radio. Not at all sure of the significance of the news coming over the airways, I, at the age of six years, and my cousin, Mary Beth, a year younger, did recognize that with the adults focused on hearing the news, this might be an opportune time to test our limits. Unnoticed, we elected to go into her bedroom and jump up and down on her bed, a practice strictly forbidden at my house, but only frowned on at Aunt Virginia's. Apparently my cousins and I were good at jumping, as 8 year old Harry was sporting a cast on his right arm. He had broken his arm a few days earlier because a friend had dared him to jump out of their hay loft. A small price to pay, for he would never back down from a dare! He wore the cast like a badge of courage.

And so it was that the news of the beginning of the United States' involvement in World War II became known to us. Our nation became inebriated with patriotism, and everyone pitched in to do his part. Victory gardens grew everywhere. Sunshine Clark (no relation) even had a tomato plant spring up in the crack of her sidewalk.

Scrap iron, and even the foil inner wrappers from chewing gum, was collected for the war effort to the chant "Save your scrap. Help sink a Jap". Many local residents allowed as how the Japanese had been able to wage this entire war thanks to the scrap iron that was donated by the United States when Japan suffered the great earthquake of 1923.

Spencer Tracey and Clark Gable thrilled the hearts of the American people as they flew through the wild blue yonder. We all slept better at night knowing they were invariably winning those Hollywood-staged battles. In those pre-television days, newsreels at the local theater kept everyone informed on the progress of the foreign war campaigns. It was about this time that I fell madly in love with Clark Gable. I thought he was so handsome with his suave moustache. I wondered why Hitler didn't pattern himself after him, instead of the paintbrush moustache he wore.

A boy in our neighborhood, Hampton Erwin, who had only recently graduated high school, learned to fly an airplane. He would fly his Piper Cub so low over our house that he cast huge shadows on the ground. My dog, Stuffy, would chase the shadows, going in circles, just like the plane did. Hampton joined the Army Air Force, where he flew fighter planes on many missions. He was eventually promoted to Colonel and received many medals by the end of the war. Col. Erwin was also a very handsome man, and Clark Gable had competition, as my crush quickly shifted to the new war hero.

Propaganda, though it wasn't called that, poured forth on the willing American people. Even the children were included in the scheme of things, reminiscent of World War I when the popular child star, Baby Peggy had encouraged the children of that day to spit on daddies who were lax in their patriotic duties. Toys, innocent in the pre-war days magically became machine guns in the hands of children, who used them to wipe out an imaginary Nazi army in one fell swoop.

Men were drafted and thousands eagerly volunteered. For who could ignore the poster with the withering look from a stern faced Uncle Sam, who, regardless of the angle ,always appeared to be looking straight at the viewer, while he pointed a judgmental finger , proclaiming "I want you". Posters appeared everywhere, among them one of Rosie the Riveter working on a Flying Fortress, symbolic of all the women who had gone to work in the defense plants and shipyards.

Everyone was cautioned not to discuss military secrets, as if anybody knew any. A popular slogan seen on many posters was "Loose Lips Sink Ships." But I was convinced of my duty along this line when I saw the newest poster, showing a sailor's uniform, permanently unoccupied, draped across an easy chair, guarded by the family dog, a gold star in the window, and across the top of the poster the guilt-provoking accusation, "Somebody talked".

Entire families gathered around their radios to respectfully listen to Franklin Delano Roosevelt speak to the nation; fireside chats, he called them. As an indication of the unity and single purpose of the American people, he always commenced these talks with "My friends…." Criticism of our Commander-in-Chief was practically unheard of in those days. Anti-war demonstrations—indeed, anti-war thoughts—were never considered.

Rationing was instituted, and tiny round tokens were issued to entitle a person to purchase items made scarce due to the channeling of certain materials to the war effort. Some people who didn't own cars might swap their gasoline tokens for someone else's precious sugar allowances. Silk, rayon, and the new nylon, formerly used in the manufacture of ladies' stockings, were among those needed materials, so American women were asked to forego these luxuries. But since necessity is the mother of invention, soon someone created liquid leg make-up, and some of the more artistic users even painted seams down the back of their legs, in keeping with the style of the day.

At school we were encouraged to buy savings stamps, which I faithfully licked and pasted in the book, which promised to turn into a mighty war bond when filled. In some mysterious way, this was supposed to hasten "bringing our boys home".

Loyalty permeated our every thought, and the whole world was categorized as either ally or enemy. One night my sister, who was a few years older than I, was studying the biography of Abraham Lincoln. I could not understand her laughter when I asked the seemingly pertinent and logical question, "Is he on our side?"

On this particular day, our school was visited by a representative from the American Red Cross. We had all assembled in the gym, where the speaker convinced us of the significance of every individual contribution.

As he talked, a lump came to my throat, and a vision of a wounded soldier, swathed in blood-stained bandages, limping, but supported by a brave comrade, came to my mind. As they trudged off the battlefield under heavy enemy fire, they were met by a heroic Red Cross worker, who eagerly ran up with outstretched arms, offering doughnuts and a hot cup of coffee—and the eternally present, life sustaining cigarette! I had noticed in the movies that when a soldier was mortally wounded and placed on a stretcher, someone always lit a cigarette and put it in his mouth. I assumed it was part of the last rites.

Then came the day that my girlfriend, Shirley and I were to ride the school bus to my grandmother's house to spend the night. Fired up by the Red Cross pep talk, we set out to give Grandma's neighbors a chance to contribute. It was just before dusk when we arrived at Mrs. Cathcart's house. We both gave a testimonial for the Red Cross, but it was my outstretched hand that received the shiny dime and nickel. Fifteen cents! I could imagine this would buy yards and yards of white bandages, or perhaps several pairs of warm woolen socks, knit by loving hands, and certainly several cartons of Camels or Lucky Strikes.

Ecstatic with our success, we were so excited we could hardly sleep that night. It was with vivid anticipation that I planned to walk to the front of Miss Hale's class and drop those two enormous coins, loudly, into the Red Cross collection can, no doubt to the envy of the other less successful first graders.

It seemed we had just dozed off when Grandma awoke us. We had to arise early, since the bus didn't come all the way to Grandma's house anymore, and we would have to walk to Taylor's Store to wait for it.

Inside the store we had time to kill, so we eagerly inspected the wares. But soon our gaze focused on the large glass case which contained a wide variety of candy bars; rationing had not yet reached Taylor's Store. There were Milky Ways, Three Musketeers, and Baby Ruths. How my mouth watered!

Shirley, a whole year older than I, and well seasoned in the way of the world, suggested how good the Baby Ruth would taste. I could almost smell the roasted peanuts, almost taste the caramel. I was so engrossed in the thought that I instinctively reached up to wipe the chocolate from my face.

The wounded soldier seemed very far away.

My friend, and now my conspirator, whispered in my ear, "We could buy three Baby Ruths with the 15 cents." But I overruled her. We bought only two Baby Ruths, and just to keep things honorable, the nickel purchased a package of candy cigarettes.

We sucked on the mint flavored chalk-white cigarettes with the bright red tips, and with a little help from the frosty air making our breath misty, blew imaginary smoke into the faces of the other passengers on the early morning school bus.

But crime doesn't pay, and the store's proprietor, suspicious at our having such a large sum of money, reported the facts to my mother, who in turn used tactics worthy of the FBI and CIA combined, came up with all the sordid details.

Knowing exactly how Benedict Arnold must have felt, I apologized to Mrs. Cathcart, made full restitution to the Red Cross, and have never tasted another Baby Ruth since. And perhaps as a means of penance, as an adult I have volunteered on two Red Cross national disasters, and my husband has been on 28. And we both donate to the Red Cross blood drive regularly. Though my blood type is so rare that less than 6 percent of the population have my type, I'm still willing to share.

CHAPTER 2: THE COUPON

Excitement was in the air as my youngest brother, Hugh Thomas (all Southerners are called by their double names), tenaciously clutching the precious coupon in his hand, climbed into the old farm truck beside Papa, who was already at the wheel. They were on the way to Wiswell, a country store that provided the necessities of life, as well as a gathering place for neighbors and friends. A trip to the store usually included participating in a game or two of checkers; this would be sitting around a pot bellied stove, if it was winter time. The coupon had come in the mail and was good for a free bottle of Pepsi-Cola, a product new to our neck of the woods at that time.

When the coupon arrived in the mailbox, the family, which included five children, selected Hugh Thomas to be the lucky consumer. In fact, though he was three years older than me, he often seemed the favored child. Perhaps it was because he had been so seriously ill the year before. Since it was a few years before the advent of antibiotics, pneumonia and its attendant raging fever had made his condition precarious. I can still remember our family doctor coming to our house, and as he stood by the sick bed listening to Hugh Thomas' chest, he shook his head gravely.

Mama, who had sat by his side day and night, attempting to sponge away his fever, got up and quietly left the room. She later said she went outside and knelt by the huge oak tree and prayed, and in her own words, "gave the child to God". Feeling a tremendous weight lifted from her shoulders, she returned to the sick room, ready to accept the outcome, whatever God's Will might be.

Aunt Omie, on the other hand, who had been filling in for Mama while she was outside praying, was not so accepting of the fate. She had found Papa's whiskey, kept solely for the occasional bedtime toddy or sure-fire cough remedy, and had filled a tablespoon with the amber liquid. She lifted Hugh Thomas' head from the pillow and poured the whiskey into his mouth. With much sputtering and coughing, which apparently dislodged a mucous plug from his trachea, he roused from his semi-comatose state. Shortly thereafter his fever broke, and he gradually regained his strength.

Mama gave the glory to God. Aunt Omie gave at least part of the credit to Jim Beam.

So now a year later, on this momentous occasion when Hugh Thomas was awarded the coupon for the free Pepsi Cola, which was worth five cents, the rest of us did not begrudge his good fortune; we were content to merely listen in awe to his later assessment of the product.

While they were at the store, Mr. Lee Humpreys, a neighbor who lived near the store, came in to redeem his Pepsi-Cola coupon. He was well known to be a dour and extremely frugal man, and he apparently did not approve of something as frivolous as soda pop, as it was later to be called. In that vein, he attempted to persuade the merchant to swap his coupon for something more practical. He said brusquely, "I would rather have a nickel curry comb" which was an item used to brush the coat of his old mule. Till this day members of my family, if presented with something less than desirable will respond with, "Well, I'd rather have a nickel curry comb".

After this, Hugh Thomas eagerly awaited the rural mail carrier each day, hoping for another stroke of good luck. But alas, it seemed that the one free offer was the end of his windfall.

But then one day Hugh Thomas became ill, complaining of a belly ache and making many trips to the out house. This brought back memories of his previous bout with pneumonia. We were all solicitous of our little brother, bowing to his every whim.

The tune changed however, when he confessed to eating the entire little box of chocolate candy that the mail man brought the day before. With a little more coercion, he produced the empty box, which to everyone's amusement was labeled EX-LAX!

CHAPTER 3: OUR
COUNTRY DOCTOR

Dr. Cody Jones, who had grown up in a nearby community and graduated from the University of Louisville Medical School, had just returned to his hometown to practice medicine. Unfortunately, soon thereafter the United States entered the Great War. At that time it was not called World War I, because it was supposed to be the war to end all wars, and therefore no one thought there would ever be a WWII. Young Dr. Jones was called to serve his country. About three months later, the Great Flu Epidemic of 1918-1919 broke out and he was given a temporary discharge so that he could return home to care for the sick. The epidemic became pandemic and killed an estimated 50 million people, maybe more. Influenza and its attendant pneumonia killed more American soldiers and sailors during the war than did enemy weapons, partly due to the crowded conditions of military camps and conditions in the trenches on the battlefields.

So Dr. Jones became our beloved country doctor who treated every malady suffered by the families in his community of Lynn Grove and the surrounding areas. He kept half of the people in the west side of Calloway County alive beyond their allotted time. In his early practice the roads were so bad that he made his house calls on horse back, and then by horse and buggy. During the depression some of his patients paid him with pigs, calves, or chickens.

As time went on he not only saw patients in his clinic, which was attached to his house, but he continued to make house calls. Later, when several of the farmers had cars, Dr. Jones was the only person whose car had two tail lights, one on each side. Consequently, if anyone heard a car coming down the road at night one of the kids would rush to the window to see if the passing car had two tail lights. If, indeed that was the case, then it was assumed that a neighbor up the road was sick. This would cause someone to get on the old telephone on the wall, ring up a neighbor, trying to determine who was ill.

One day Iva Nel, who was three years old, was bitten on her ear by a dog, an incident that instilled in her a life-long fear of dogs. Papa took her to Dr. Jones' office, where he sewed it up, and he gave her a nickel when he finished. They stopped at Wiswell on the way home for her to spend her windfall. She bought chewing gum, but found it hurt her ear to chew it, so she grudgingly gave the gum to Rebecca. Rebecca recalled that she longed to be bitten by a dog so she could go see Dr. Jones, receive a nickel, and receive solicitous care like her sister.

In 1933 his house and office caught on fire. As it burned, Dr. Jones stayed in his office passing medicines out the window to the men and boys who had rushed to the scene from nearby Lynn Grove High School to help, directed by the Principal Buron "Boots" Jeffrey. Dr. Jones temporarily moved his practice to Murray but rebuilt his house and office at the previous location a few years later.

When a woman was pregnant she would visit Dr. Jones in his clinic, primarily to determine a due date. Unless major complications arose, the doctor would not be called again until time to come to the home for the delivery. He would bring "Miss Annie", his wife, who was skilled as his assistant at childbirth. While Dr. Jones was a compassionate physician, he had no tolerance for lassitude. He said that the parents had nine months to choose a name for the expected baby. Therefore he expected to be informed of the name when he signed the birth certificate immediately following the delivery. And if no name was given, he apparently saw it as his duty to fill in the blank himself. A neighboring couple had not agreed on a name for their newborn son, but ultimately named him Charles, Jr. Eighteen years later he was drafted into the army, which required him to produce his birth certificate. To his great embarrassment, he discovered that his legal first name was Lucy! I, myself, was named Malinda at birth, but whether Dr. Jones misunderstood, or just disliked the name, or quite possibly because it was 2 o'clock on a very cold February morning, my birth certificate proclaimed Linda as my name, and so it has been ever since.

In that day and age babies were welcomed and cherished as part of the family, but perhaps also seen as prospective help on the farms. One of the neighbors, Betsy, saw that Dr. Jones had been to the Barrett's house just up the road where a baby was due. She got on the telephone and called other ladies on the line until she found out that her suspicions of what was happening was correct. Shortly after, she went out to the field where her husband George, was plowing. She told him, "I talked to Clara on the telephone and she said the Barretts had a new baby. Now we must be polite and go get a look at the new baby. I don't want to be the last woman to go see them:. "Lawsy me," he spat his tobacco juice. "If I unhitched this mule and took out to visit every time Polly Barrett had a young 'un, why I'd never get a crop out!"

CHAPTER 4: THE
NEW PREACHER

———◆———

The old phrase "as poor as a church mouse" could have been originated especially as a description of our new preacher, Brother Lawrence. He and his family had been "called" to Sinking Spring Baptist Church, which served as our place of worship, but was also called the "meeting house". After services the members stood in groups on the church steps or in the parking lot, socializing. There was a different denominational church a few miles away, and despite the differences in theology, both churches were careful to plan their summer revivals at alternate times so the entire community could attend services at both churches, Our church was a white wooden building. The other church, South Pleasant Grove Methodist, was a newer brick building. The Wilkerson children were discussing their preferences and Rebecca especially wanted to attend the brick church. "I don't want to go to that old plank church", was how she said it.

Not only was our new preacher's family poor, but so were most members of the congregation in this little farming community. The country was still trying to recover from the great depression and though the new preacher was dependent on the church members for his livelihood he could not expect much monetary compensation. When he visited in our home as part of his pastoral duties, he would often leave with the gift of a freshly dressed frying chicken, a dozen eggs, and some fresh vegetables in season.

When Bro. Lawrence came for his trial sermon, his wife Eva, their daughter Eulala, and son, Donald accompanied him. Afterwards the deacons recommended that he be extended an invitation to become our pastor, and the congregation, being a democratic body, voted affirmatively. As part payment for his service they were allowed to live in one of the member's house formerly occupied by a share cropper.

Shortly after their arrival and getting settled into their new home, the members decided to give them the traditional "Pounding". This was a welcoming event and was an effort to make them feel at home. It was called a Pounding because each family brought a pound of such things as home-made butter, sugar, flour, lard, sweet potatoes, molasses, turnips, or whatever they had grown or prepared and was presented to the new preacher after that first Sunday night service.

The preacher's family fit right in to the community and was looked upon fondly by the membership. During the next summer when it was time for the first revival, Mrs. Eva was very anxious that her little family would make a good impression on the visiting evangelist. Though he was put up at the home of a deacon for the duration of the time he was conducting the revival, he was invited to have supper at the pastor's home one night. Mrs. Eva got out the good red and white checked oil cloth tablecloth and gave her mis-matched dining chairs an extra polishing. She was very embarrassed at her lack of nice cutlery, but she made sure the guest had the china plate, as well as a knife and fork. She attempted to pass off her embarrassment by saying, "I just don't know where all my spoons have gotten to". To her consternation her son piped with, "Here's both of them."

CHAPTER 5: THE RED CRAYON

I was the youngest of five children and for many years I was left behind when the older siblings boarded the school bus every morning. I was a very finicky eater, and therefore very skinny, which concerned my mother, who prided herself on her cooking. One morning my sisters packed their lunches and placed them on the swing on the front porch awaiting the bus. Suddenly I had an overwhelming urge to eat a peanut butter sandwich, so when their backs were turned I opened the lunch box and helped myself. I was not aware of the joy this gave my mother—to see me eat. I was also not aware of the many times thereafter that a "decoy" lunch was placed on the front porch swing to tempt me.

But at last I was finally old enough to ride that big yellow school bus myself. I felt so grown up. The school bus was very old and quite dilapidated. The reason that it kept running, I heard, was that the bus driver, Vernon Jackson, was also a skilled mechanic and worked on it as needed. Not only the bus, but also the rural gravel roads were sometimes in bad shape, and were tended by the local residents rather than a highway department. For a time the big bridge at Wiswell was considered too unstable to support the weight of the big bus full of kids. So Mr. Jackson would stop as he approached the bridge, and let all the kids out. He would drive the empty bus across the bridge, and then the children would walk across, and re-board the bus. We thought this a regular treat and so looked forward to this occurrence as we went to, and again from, school.

This was many years before the institution of the "No child left behind" initiative, and three of my classmates were indeed left behind, that is they flunked the first grade. Also this was years before teachers were taught to protect young first graders' fragile self images. Miss Hale, our prim first grade teacher devised a method of punishment I have never heard of since. She created a "cat tail" by taking a length of wire, padding it, and then covering it with a furry fabric. When a child misbehaved according to her strict standards, the cat tail was pinned on his derriere and was worn out during recess. Oh how I longed for the attention that wearing the cat tail afforded. But I was never quite sure what criteria were required to qualify for the honor. Besides, Bobby Kemp seemed to have the privilege sewn up! One day he even got to wear the cat tail on the bus all the way home. I was unsure why the older kids laughed at him or why he seemed so humiliated.

In those days children were not usually taught to read before starting to school and teachers had to start from scratch. But my sisters had taught me to read at home. Our principal, Mr. Jeffery was so impressed that he had me read the "Dick and Jane" book backwards to be certain that I had not just memorized it. When I returned home from my first day of school my father asked me what I had learned. I responded with, "Nothing. I already know it all". When I learned that by adding an s or es to a word would make it plural I decided that to call a single piece of clothing "clothes" was superfluous; one item should simply be a "clo".

It had been a big day when my mother and I had shopped for my first school supplies. This consisted of a little jar of paste, small blunt edged scissors, a "rough leaf" tablet (we would not get the more expensive "slick leaf" tablets until the fourth grade), a small box of crayons that we called "colors" and one yellow No. 2 pencil with eraser. The eraser was destined to be used quite regularly. The pencil itself was rather short-lived thanks to repeated trips to the corner of the room to use the manual pencil sharpener attached to the wall there. Pencil sharpening was one of the few legitimate reasons for arising from our seats that met with the strict approval of Miss Hale. Unfortunately for Nancy Hope, the littlest child in our class, going to the bathroom was not necessarily an approved activity. Consequently, the cat tail was sometimes attached to her wet pants.

There were three little tables in our classroom, and six little chairs at each table. They had been constructed by our teacher's father, and he had painted them a bright red. We were allowed to choose our chair which was then assigned to us permanently. My table mates were all girls. Across from us was a table with six boys, who would rather have died than have had to sit at a table with a girl. I learned the boys were named Max, Kelvin, Lloyd, Johnny, and two Bobbys; Bobby Kemp, who was seldom at the table but could be found sitting in the corner , an early version of "time out", and Bobby Frank, who would later be recognized as Valedictorian of our graduating senior class.

I kept my colors in a match box that had a cover that slid out. The more affluent students, who had larger hoards of colors, kept them in cigar boxes. As the year wore on the colors wore down. My red color, my favorite, was almost entirely used up. What to do? Ruth, the student across the table from me, had an impressive supply of colors, though she came from the most poverty stricken family in the community. I noticed that she had TWO red colors. Why would anyone need two red colors? Why should anyone have two while someone (me) had practically NONE? A plan began to formulate in my mind. I needed a conspirator. I tapped my friend, Lilly for this activity, though she had no idea of my intention. When recess came I instructed Lilly to detain Ruth on the playground. No one noticed I lingered in the classroom. I picked up Ruth's matchbox and then sat it back down. I went to the window to make sure no one was heading back inside. I could see Marie and Ann tossing the jump rope, while Lou Ann jumped in cadence to a little ditty that we had made up.: "I have a boyfriend; I won't tell; he eats peanuts; but not the shells; he can jump; but he can't dance; 'cause he's got a hole; in his old pants". I could still hear their giggling as I returned to our little table and picked up Ruth's match box again. My palms were sweaty. I was breathing hard. With much trepidation I opened the box. With furtive glances I made sure no one was watching me. I reached in and grasped a red color. In my defense I took the shortest one; one that already had the paper covering peeled off. I did not know how close I had come to qualifying for wearing the coveted cat tail.

But no one ever found out about my heinous act. Perhaps my conscience was eased somewhat by the fact that Ruth apparently never missed the superfluous red color. Yet with the passage of time I have never forgotten my transgression.

I believe Ruth and her family moved away a year or so later and I never saw her again. So now, seventy-something years later, Ruth Fowler, sister of Deletha Jean Fowler, wherever you are, I am truly sorry.

CHAPTER 6: LITTLE AZZIE

Though Queen Victoria, Queen of England and Ireland, died in 1901, the Victorian style of modesty still prevailed in the little rural community of Wiswell in Weestern Kentucky in the 1920s. In conversation one would never use the suggestive term "leg" but instead would say "limb". The more modern and daring might go so far as to say "lower limb". Men were very careful not to offend the delicate sensitivity of women when in mixed company.

Wiswell, being a farming community, when harvest time came around, the neighboring farmers worked together, moving from one farm to another. They would all get together at one farm, picking the corn, threshing the wheat, or baling the hay—whatever crop was ready at the time, until every family's farm work was completed. Later when the weather was cold, with the same joint work plan, hogs were butchered; hams and bacon were cured and hung in the smoke house, and stored for the upcoming year.

All the wives would congregate at the host farm where they would help prepare a sumptuous meal for the hard working men. The noon meal was called dinner, and never referred to as lunch, and each woman tried to out do the others when it was her turn to have the meal at her house. The men were always served at the "first table" while the women "waited on" them. After the men returned to work, the women and children would eat.

One cool fall day during the wheat threshing at the Deck Paschall farm, the men had just entered the dining room for their dinner. Mr. Paschall's young daughter, Azzie, was lying on the rug in front of the fireplace with a Sears-Roebuck catalog open in front of her. Everyone was admiring the lovely child. Someone asked if she was choosing something from the catalog for Santa to bring her for Christmas. Her father was a very shy and easily embarrassed man, and to his mortification, in front of all his neighbors, he heard little Azzie announce loudly, "My daddy just loves to look in this catalog at the women in their union suits!"

CHAPTER 7: LITTLE AZZIE GREW UP

———◆———

And little Azzie did grow up, and she married her high school sweetheart, Walzie Lewis. In fact they got married as soon as they graduated, as the United States had just entered WWII and his induction into the armed forces was almost certain. They did not want to wait.

As was the custom in their community they would live with his or her parents the first year so they could save up enough money to establish a home of their own. Walzie was classified as 1-A with the draft board, and on his 19th birthday he was called to come for his physical exam, which he passed with flying colors. He then received his orders to report to Fort Knox for six weeks basic training, and from there he would be sent overseas to parts unknown to engage in battles to preserve our freedom.

With much sadness and many tears the young couple clung to each other until the conductor shouted the last "all aboard". Walzie jumped onto the train, which had already started to pull away. Azzie ran along side the train, waving her white lace handkerchief, as Walzie, having to lean over several other soldiers who were already seated, waved back at her. Though it was a bright sunshiny day, flowers were in bloom, and birds were chirping, the world looked dull and drab to Azzie, as she sobbed into her white lace handkerchief.

Azzie returned to her parents' home where she and her mother grew a "victory garden", growing vegetables for canning, as there were rumors that all kinds of things were going to be rationed. This rumor soon became a fact, and tokens were doled out for everything from sugar to gasoline, in limited supplies. No one really complained, because they felt that the more they sacrificed the sooner the war would be won, and the soldier boys would be coming home.

Azzie volunteered with the Red Cross and took training as a nursing aide to be ready to care for any wounded soldier who might be brought back to her hometown for treatment. She did in fact, work in the local hospital, allowing some of the trained nurses to join up and be shipped overseas where wounded soldiers were treated.

Walzie wrote letters to Azzie as often as possible, though she had no idea where he was as each of his letters were read by a censor before being sent, and any hint as to his location (or any other information that might be of interest to the enemy), was actually cut out of the letter. But his declarations of love, his dreams of the future, his longing to see his young bride, were all left intact. Azzie wrote him faithfully and looked forward to the day they would be reunited.

And finally, three years later that day finally came. She put on her new blue dress, the only new dress she had bought during the war. Styles had changed lately and dresses were much shorter, since fabric was in short supply, and manufacturers were focused on making soldiers' uniforms rather than clothing for civilians. If only she had some nylon stockings, she thought, but nylon was all designated as material for parachutes. Her shoes had been polished and shined, though quite worn, but she had no token to buy new ones.

She looked at herself in the mirror as she adjusted her hat, tilting it a little to the side, just like Lana Turner and Betty Grable did theirs in the Hollywood movies where they starred with Jimmy Stewart and Clark Gable in such movies as "Thirty Minutes Over Tokyo" and the latest hit "Coming in on a Wing and a Prayer"; war movies meant to inspire patriotism and soften the blow of rationing and scarcity of products that had been plentiful and taken for granted in pre-war days.

So here she was, at the train depot, awaiting the same train to bring her husband home that had taken him away. When he stepped off the train she thought he was so handsome in his uniform. Though much thinner, he actually was taller than when she last saw him.

After all the months and months of waiting with anxiety and worry about his well being, he was finally safely home! She ran to him, they kissed and embraced. He swept her off her feet, twirling her around. She looked into his eyes and said, "I sure am going to miss your letters!"

CHAPTER 8: FAMILY CHICKENS

———◆———

Chickens played a big role in making our farm life self sufficient. They provided eggs, as well as being the source of Mama's delectable fried chicken—fried in lard, of course—to say nothing of her chicken and dressing or delicious dumplin's . She always said her favorite pieces of the chicken were the neck and the back. That might be the only pieces she ever tasted, for with five children to feed that's probably all that was left.

When the chickens became frying size, Mama would take the selected one to the chopping block, lay its head thereon, and with one swoop of the very sharp hatchet decapitate the unsuspecting fryer. She would then toss it on the ground where it would continue to flop and move around for several seconds. She thought this swift method was more humane than some of our heartless neighbors who actually wrung the neck until the head came off. We kids were always dismayed and felt such sympathy for the chicken—but we got over it by supper time.

The nice soft feathers were used in feather beds and fluffy pillows.

But Mama's chickens represented much more than their contribution to the food chain. In the early spring we would occasionally find a setting hen in some obscure hiding place where she had saved up some of her own eggs in a make-shift nest. The hen's maternal instinct was so strong that nothing could persuade her to leave the nest. .If the nest was not discovered, the end result might be the new mother hen come strutting into the chicken yard with her baby chickens following close behind. But Mama purposely provided nests in the hen house for setting hens, where they'd be safe from predators, such as wild animals, most notably foxes, as well as the neighbor's "egg sucking" dogs. Sometimes, when the quota for baby chicks was filled, there would be hens with such a strong desire for motherhood that they would have to be placed in lock-up until the urge to set waned

But if these hatchings didn't replenish the chicken population at our house, Mama would order baby chicks from a mail order company. It was always a great adventure to discuss and decide which breed of chickens to order. Maybe domineckers, with their black and white checked feathers, and who were known to be good layers. Leghorns might be a good choice, though they were smaller boned, but meaty. Perhaps the sturdy Plymouth Rock, or maybe the large Rhode Island Reds, which as their name suggested had beautiful shiny red feathers that just sparkled in the sunshine Their amazing attribute was the highly desirable brown eggs that they laid, which contained darker yellow yolks, which were presumed to be richer in protein. We always had a few bantam chickens, which were miniature versions of the larger birds. We called them "Banties" and they were primarily kept as pets, though they did produce tiny eggs, which added food to our larder.

The rural mail carrier, seemed to me to detest children, annoyed by how we sometimes jumped up on his running board before he came to a full stop, with hands outstretched hoping to receive a letter from one of our sisters who had escaped farm drudgery by emigrating to the big city of Detroit to work in the defense plants. However he would bring the baby chicks in heavy cardboard boxes with holes punched in the side to allow ventilation so the chicks could breathe. The inside of the box held fine wood shavings for the chicks to rest on and scratch in. When they arrived all of the kids came and were mesmerized when viewing the tiny creatures covered in delicate yellow down. No one was more enchanted with the baby chicks than Mama. She loved those baby chickens and would talk baby talk to them. In response they would increase their peeping sounds and actually gather at the side of the box nearest where Mama stood. Sometimes there would be a baby or two who succumbed to the hazards of the trip, and after many expressions of sorrow, the children would place the little corpses in a shoe box and after proper ceremony bury it in the back yard. Most of the time the weather was still too cool and the new chicks were too young to join the older chickens outside, so they were kept in their box and placed in a warm space behind our big wood burning cook stove, making an incubator, of sorts. In addition to baby chicken feed, Mama would hard boil a couple eggs and mash them finely and feed it to the babies. This made me wonder if feeding eggs to the chickens might be considered cannibalism,

It was interesting to see how many turned out to be roosters and how many were pullets. Pullets were destined to become valued laying hens; roosters were mainly destined for the frying pan. When the pullets first began to lay, the eggs were quite small, but as the hens grew, the size of the eggs increased. When occasionally there was an egg with a double yolk, we kids all came running to view this phenomenon.

I will have to admit as valuable as the chickens were to us, they were not the smartest creatures in the barnyard. Once we had a violent hail storm that came without warning. Our new ingenious neighbors had devised a plan for some extra income by planting a large field of tomatoes, and securing a contract for shipping the ripe tomatoes to the canning factory. They were almost ready for picking when this storm came and the entire crop of tomatoes were crushed and destroyed. We found many of our young pullets in a huddled mass against one end of the pen. The pen had a roof, so the hail did not kill them, but rather they suffocated because they had panicked and piled up so tightly they couldn't breathe, and did not recognize the folly of their ways.

One of my brother Hugh's chores was to feed the pigs their supper each night. He would throw ears of corn over into the pig pen. Several chickens saw this as a means to help themselves to some of the loose grains and so managed to get into the pen to enjoy the pickings. Hugh accidently hit one of the chickens with an ear of corn, and knocked it out cold. He picked it up, began to rub it briskly and it revived. He took it to the house, wrapped it in a towel and laid it on a pillow on the porch. The next morning it was able to ambulate, and we noticed it followed Hugh everywhere he went. Hugh taught it to perch on his shoulder and it would stay there for extended periods of time. Hugh could be seen riding his bicycle all over the neighborhood with his pet chicken riding on his shoulder, reminiscent of a pirate and his parrot.

While Hugh's chicken was very docile, my grandmother had a huge vicious rooster, who was known to "flog" the unwary person traveling too close to his territory. He had sharp spurs on the back of his legs that he used to dig into his victim, which could cause serious injury. I was just a little girl during his rule of the hen yard, but he developed a particular dislike for me, and my granddaddy had to rescue me more than once. The rooster finally met my grandmother's roasting pan, restoring peace to the vicinity, though some of the hens seemed a little frustrated.

My grandmother was a wonderful southern cook, and fried chicken was her specialty. When her little four year old great-grandson from Michigan came to visit, she was helping him select food from her bountiful supper. She asked, "James, what part of the chicken do you want?" She meant drumstick, wing, etc. He thought a moment and said, "I believe I'll have the dominecker part".

Every spring Mama gave the older children some "cleansing" medicine. She believed that a cathartic would refresh the gastrointestinal system, whet the appetite, and just improve the bodily constitution. When Iva Nel was given her pills, she waited until Mama had gone on to other chores. She tossed her pills into the back yard, and then gleefully watched as the chickens fought over the strange looking pellets. Lucky for me, Mama had abandoned this practice before I came along.

A peddler who drove his truck stuffed with household goods came by our house each Friday. Mama always tried to buy something, though we raised almost everything we ate. She usually paid for her purchases by selling a dozen or two of her eggs, or occasionally she'd sell a hen, especially if the hen had become a little lax in her egg laying duties. The peddler man carried a chicken coop on the outside back of the truck just for transporting the hens that he had bartered for. He weighed the fowl by tying a cord around its feet so that he could attach the spring scales and hold it up to weigh it.

How times have changed since Mama's day: I remember Mama lamenting to a neighbor, "Why the only thing you can buy for a nickel these days is a box of Arm and Hammer baking soda". Then later when she was less able to garden and needed to supplement her own produce by way of shopping in the grocery store, she said in an incredible tone of voice, "I spent $5 on groceries today and it all fit in one bag!"

We had a new neighbor move into the neighborhood from somewhere up north, and she was trying to get a brood of chickens established. We noticed she was not very familiar with the country life style, and, shall I say quite naïve in other aspects. Mama and I visited her in her home one day. I was wondering how her chicken enterprise was going, so I asked her how many chickens she had. She hesitated a moment and then said, "I'm just not sure. I counted 19 this morning but one ran around the house so fast I couldn't count it".

CHAPTER 9: JOETTE, MY FRIEND

Yes, Joette became my best friend on that fateful first day in the first grade at Lynn Grove School, when a mischievous little boy, a fellow classmate, pulled my little chair out from under me causing me to sit in the floor. Joette helped me up and our friendship was cemented from that day forward.

Joette lived in a community called Protemus, and had to walk out to the general store to meet the school bus, as the road to her house would often be impassable, especially in rainy or snowy weather, and the school bus couldn't get through.

I lived in the Wiswell farming community, which also had a country store. Joette and I spent many over-nights at one or the other's house, and when Shirley moved into my neighborhood, the three of us became fast friends and called ourselves the Lynn Grove Trio. Sometimes we walked the two miles from my house to the Wiswell store where we bought huge RC Colas in glass bottles and little bags of peanuts, which we emptied into the colas, and finished off on our two mile trek back home.

Joette loved to write and her talent became apparent at a very early age. At about age 9, she contacted the editor of our weekly newspaper proposing to write a weekly column of the news in her neighborhood, titled "Protemus Palaver". She was hired as a "stringer", which meant the length of her column was measured by a string of known length and she was paid according to how much newspaper space was occupied by her writing. She was paid 5 cents per inch and received a complementary copy of the paper. Since she had access to the news she visited some elderly couples in the neighborhood, who did not have a radio or newspaper and kept them informed about the ongoing WWII. She was quite up to date and knowledgeable about the Allies and the Nazis.

Then at age 11, she branched out from just writing the local news and added a column called, "Children's Stories" that she composed entirely by herself. Through these enterprises she managed to have a little spending money, but she did have to buy her own shoes. Unfortunately shoes didn't last long traipsing through the rutted and muddy Protemus roads. (Ironically in this present day, there is a nice paved road through there and several large beautiful homes have been built on lovely landscaped lawns. Her old home has been torn down but the owners of that property had the foresight to salvage a little log cabin which had been the kitchen portion of her former home, keeping it pretty much intact, as in its original state.)

As children, we decided that since we were going to be best friends for life we might as well make it official. So Joette wrote up a friendship contract, and to make it especially binding we agreed to sign it in blood. She found an ordinary straight pin, stuck her finger and signed it in blood. I, however, chickened out.

Our friend, Shirley lived in a farmhouse back in the woods approximately a mile from me, and we had to travel through the woods by walking down a little lane. Sometimes when she visited me I would accompany her part way to her house, estimating when we had gone half-way. We decided we needed to know exactly where the half-way point was. So we counted every step from my house to hers. Then we turned around and counted half that number of steps and declared that to be half way, and erected a sign marking that fact.

One day when the 3 of us were at Shirley's we decided we would form an exclusive club. Jettye Jo, Shirley's older sister, informed us that all clubs had to have mascots. So what to do? What would be an appropriate mascot? Jettye Jo remembered there was a nest of baby birds in a hollow knot hole in a tree in the back yard. She volunteered to retrieve one of the baby birds to fulfill the role of our club mascot. We waited until the mother bird left the nest in search of a worm for her babies' dinner. Jettye Jo approached the big knot hole, as the rest of us watched in awe of her fearsome task. She reached into the hollow tree and far below grasped a little bird in her fist. But when she tried to pull the bird out, her arm was stuck! She kept trying to remove her arm and the bird but it would not budge. She screamed and we all panicked. I ran into the house, excitedly telling their mother, that Jettye Jo's arm was stuck in the tree. Mrs. Winstead grabbed a dishpan, filled it with soapy water and ran out and poured it over Jettye Jo's arm and around the knot hole, thinking it would make things slippery and help her arm slide out. She finally realized that Jettye Jo had tenaciously held on to the little bird in her fist. Once she finally turned loose of the bird, her fist was released making the diameter smaller, and her arm easily came out. I don't know how the baby birds fared but they must have been very clean, whatever their fate.

But we all grew up and got married. Shirley eventually moved to California, where she was a multi-county librarian; Joette moved to Ohio, where she was a fourth grade teacher for over 30 years; I remained in Kentucky, teaching at Murray State University, except for brief stints elsewhere. And then one year a get together of the Lynn Grove Trio was planned at my house. Shirley, her mother and Joette were coming. But then a friend of Joette's who was going on a tour to Turkey became ill and unable to make the trip. It was too late to cancel so she offered the entire trip to Joette, all expenses paid, which was at the same time as our planned reunion. She was torn between the two options but she knew the trip to Turkey was a once in a lifetime opportunity, so she opted for the trip.

This is the letter she wrote explaining her decision: "All of life is full of choices, and I chose the 'exotic' thing to do…Istanbul, Ephsesus, Ankara, Mt. Ararat, etc. But I'm not entirely sure that is more exotic than a trip back fifty something years. I am not sure I chose wisely and I feel many pangs. I think about the three of us; you, Shirley, and I, and what charmed lives we led in many ways. Three little girls, living in the backwoods of Kentucky. We were smart kids. I think we knew that. We were not streetwise, as kids are today, but we were aware in so many ways, and open to learning. We were interested in the whole world. I think about the games we played, using mainly our imagination. I remember the night at Shirley's when we played out in the front yard---all of us. Shirley's mom and dad played with us, by the light of the moon; they were as inventive and playful as we were. How young they must have been! It's my idea of joy being created from nothing...we needed no props, just the pleasure of accepting one another, and giving in to pure child-like delight. We held hands in a circle, playing 'Drop the handkerchief'. We ran on the dew-wet grass, and I have never felt a more secure sense of well being, of the absolute rightness of the world than I did that night. That picture is so much like something from *Little House on the Prairie* . I think as they moved away from there Shirley must have said, 'And that's the last time we saw that little house'.

"Linda, I remember having a crush on your brother, Hugh. I recall feeling a sort of envy because you had beautiful older sisters, and I only had brothers, who paid me no attention. I also recall a single light bulb at the top of the stairs at your house that burned for years. That was special to me, for there were no light bulbs at my house. Or telephone. Or running water.

"One of my favorite memories of you and I, Linda, is of our struggle to understand what was going on in our pubescent bodies. I don't know about Shirley's mother, but your mother and mine were too modest to tell us about what was happening, so we put our bits and pieces together to try to make sense of it. What we came up with was a very flawed concept of sexuality. We had invented code words for everything. Remember that menstruation was "yammering". It was years before I knew that was actually a word that meant 'talking senselessly'. We wouldn't dare speak the word 'pregnant' aloud, but called it P.G. One day we were between the high school building and the gym waiting for our buses, when you pulled me aside. 'Joette', you whispered. 'Do you know that there are babies born without any fathers? They're called Bastards'. I nodded solemnly. 'Well,' you continued to whisper. 'Lately my stomach has been real hard and it's getting bigger. You know that happens when you're P.G. I think I'm going to have a Bastard'.

"Shirley was gone before we reached that stage. She had to work through her coming of age with other friends. I have wonderful memories of her. One that stands out is walking down that long lane to their little house in the woods. Jettye Jo was with us, and I was so thrilled that a big sister would pay attention to us. In my mind's eye I can see that shady track, and how we crossed the creek, I remember how demure Jettye Jo was, while we cavorted like young puppies, off the path and on again. And I remember the last time I saw Shirley, but she has always been with me, for I named my little sister after her.

"I'm so grateful for my childhood. I'm so grateful for parents, who only had love to give, but gave it, in their own very conservative way. I was always aware that they thought I could do anything I chose. I am grateful for kerosene lamps, and water drawn from a cistern, and cold winter nights huddled together in front of a wood burning fireplace. Most of all I am grateful for friends, for lovely memories that weave the tapestry of the past; for a small school where we were like family. We didn't necessarily like everybody in our class, but we knew them. We understood them. We even accepted them for who they were. That's a centering kind of thing that allows for growth, I believe the word is security. Even the throes of war that didn't quite touch us, but somehow overshadowed us could not take that away. Most of all I'm grateful for a benevolent God who must smile as life spins out with its surprises and twists.

"So since I won't be there for the Lynn Grove Trio reunion, I jealously hope you will allow me to be with you in spirit. The poem I add is one I wrote many years ago, but it somehow seems appropriate."

Love, Joette

Friendship is not nailed to time
It's fluid like the sea
It stretches to embrace the place
When you are far from me
It isn't caught in Sunday dress
All stiff, with airs too good
But, daily clothes itself with joy
Adapts its mode to mood

Friendship doesn't rust with age
It's made of stainless steel
And distance doesn't dull its blade
Or rough the edge we feel
It's hardy, and of sturdy stock
Built strong for heavy duty
But, still, ironically enough
It has a fragile beauty

— Joette McDonald

CHAPTER 10: WISHING FOR A BABY SISTER

I hated being the youngest of five children, and oh how I longed to have a baby sister! A brother, not so much, having two older brothers already, who teased me unmercifully. When they played soft ball they wouldn't let me join in the game, but they were more than happy to let me chase the errant balls and return them. Then they would laugh and call me "Little Hind Catcher". Later, in adulthood they would have great admiration for my medical knowledge, often benefitting from a consultation and medical advice. They even elected me as the first (and only) Mayor of Wiswell, by acclamation. But back to my longing for a baby sibling. Any baby would make me happy.

I sometimes day dreamed of having a baby sister and imagined what fun that would be. After all, my best friend Joette had recently gotten a baby sister, and her mother even let her name the baby. She named her Shirlee after our mutual friend, Shirley Winstead, and being creative she spelled it S-h-i-r-l-e-e. Then another friend, Rachel, who lived just up the road, got a baby sister. I suggested they name her after me, as it appeared that no new baby was forthcoming at my house, and they actually did. She was called Reda Fay. Reda, after her daddy, Reed, and Fay for me. When Reda grew up she often thanked me profusely for my input, as the alternative name would have been Reda Florence, which she felt would be entirely too old fashioned.

Shirley Temple was an extremely popular child star at that point in time, and apparently had a great influence on mothers' naming their newborns. There was a plethora of little girls named Shirley. My little friend, Shirley Ann Hill was one of them. Her daddy got her a little Shetland pony. It was through some kind of program whereby the pony could be taken to your home and the children could treat it as their own. They had to feed it and care for it until its foal would be born in the spring. Then both animals would be returned to the owner. Shirley Ann and I would take turns riding the pony. That was so much fun. So I started begging Papa to get a pony for me, as there were some more available. That would have fulfilled my two greatest desires: a pony and a baby, albeit an equine baby. But Papa refused. He was still smarting from the financial losses suffered during the depression, and he was afraid something might happen to the pony and he would be held accountable. Then to my great distress, Shirley Ann's mother went to the hospital and came home with a real baby. "Shirley Ann has it all," I thought. "A pony, a new colt on the way, and now a real baby at her house". But my jealousy disappeared when we went to see the new baby. It was just a baby brother!

I gave up on the pony, but decided to concentrate my efforts on getting a real baby. I decided to take things into my own hands and see if I could make my dream come true. Mama was sitting in a chair outside in the shade of the Hickory tree peeling apples and slicing them to put on cardboard trays to place in the sun to dry. She would use them to make her delicious fried apple pies that winter. I walked up to her and thinking to plead my case, but starting first with the basics, I said, "Mama, where do babies come from?" She dropped her knife, looked startled, and said simply, "I don't know". So that was the problem! She didn't know. No wonder I never got a baby sister since she didn't even know where they came from. Getting the five of us must have just been pure luck. And apparently she never learned, or at least she never explained it to me. I learned little bits and pieces from friends. In fact when Reda Fay was born, Rachel, who was all of seven years old, learned some of the facts of life. One fact that she confided to me, smug in her new knowledge, was if there was going to be a new baby coming you could tell because the daddy's beard would grow longer and thicker. Scientific facts, like that. I kept a close watch on Papa's beard. It never grew longer or thicker. So Rachel's information must have been correct, because the baby sister never came.

CHAPTER 11: MY BRACELET

———◆———

When Rebecca and Iva Nel were deemed old enough to go out with boys, their dates consisted of going with a parent-investigated-and-approved boy to Sunday night church services. If the dating became a little more serious it might include Wednesday night prayer meetings, also at church. Other options were well chaperoned play parties at home or at friends' houses. When Rebecca became serious about her beau, Fred, Mama invited him to a family supper.

Mama was a wonderful cook, and her homemade light and fluffy biscuits were part of every breakfast, and delicious cornbread accompanied every other meal. If we should have had to eat any other kind of bread it would have been an unthinkable hardship. But because Rebecca had a suitor coming to supper Mama wanted to appear more sophisticated so she purchased a loaf of "store-boughten" bread. And yes, there was sliced bread back then.

I was cautioned to be on my best behavior that night because it seemed they thought if I was otherwise it might foil all my sister's nuptial chances and doom her to spinsterhood. That night, with Fred ensconced at the family dining table, some of the snow white loaf bread slices, which had been placed on a plate, was passed around. Papa was asking Fred about his future plans and Fred replied with appropriate answers, acceptable from a future son-in-law. All was going well. So far, so good.

Then I reached out, took a slice of the foreign bread, bit a hole in the very center, stuck my arm through it, held up my bread encircled arm, and loudly invited everyone to see my new bracelet. While no one died of embarrassment, I think it was pretty close. Despite the apparent aberrant family member, (that would be me), Fred and Rebecca became engaged, and Fred was drafted into the Army. Rebecca went to Detroit to work in the defense plants, and when Fred returned from fighting many battles in the European conflicts, they were married and lived happily ever after.

Iva Nel was not immune to my boyfriend-alienating tactics either. I had a new puppy that accompanied me everywhere I went. Iva Nel was sitting beside her boyfriend on the sofa in the parlor. I went to their door and tossed my little puppy into the room. The boyfriend asked in a benevolent tone of voice, "What kind of dog is this?" To Iva Nel's chagrin, I replied, "It's a Spitz, and he spits just like you do." Iva Nel did get married, but not to that boy. I don't know how much my actions contributed to that outcome.

CHAPTER 12: MY BIRTH

———◆———

I asked my sister, Rebecca, to tell me what she remembered about my birth. Since she was almost 12 years old at that time I thought she would have a good memory of that momentous event. She agreed but first she wanted to tell me about how she learned there was a baby on the way. She said, "Mama told me she was going to take some tomatoes to our closest neighbor, Mrs. Windsor. Errands like that were usually my job, and I loved doing them as it was much better than working in the field. So I was sorely disappointed when she insisted on doing it herself. She combed her hair and put on a loose fitting dress, and though there wasn't supposed to be a belt, she got a piece of twine and tied around her waist. Later I learned that was the unspoken way of announcing a pregnancy, as that word was never spoken,

"Mrs. Windsor was chosen to be the first to learn of the impending birth because she was a highly respected lady, and because she could be counted on to inform all the neighbors.

"I could hardly wait for the baby to come. Iva Nel and I wanted you to be a girl so bad. I kept telling Mama I hoped she would name you Martha Josephine, but by the time you were born I had changed my mind and was begging her to name you Delores. Then I had a great idea! I suggested that we all write the name that we would choose on slips of paper, fold them, and put them in a basket. Then we would let you, a newborn baby, reach in and grab one of the papers, and that would be your name.

"When you were born, Mama told Dr. Jones your name was Malinda Fay, but when the birth certificate came it was just Linda Fay. Mama wanted to change it to Malinda but Papa wanted to leave it. I think it cost $2.00 to make a correction on a birth certificate, and that may have been a factor in the decision.

"But your name remained Linda Fay. We kids took care of you more than Mama did. You were our doll."

Lucky me!

CHAPTER 13: THE DIVIDED SKIRT

———◆———

My two sisters, Rebecca and Iva Nel, were 15 and 13 years old, respectively and due to the fact that Iva Nel had been promoted ahead by two grades, they were in the same class. They were looking forward to their annual end of the school year field trip. This year the class would be going to the historic Columbus-Belmont State Park, located a couple counties over, a site that figured prominently in the Civil War. They had studied about the huge anchor and attached massive chain on display on the banks of the Mississippi River. The Confederates had placed the chain across the river, fixing it in place with the anchor, to impede the river traffic of the Union Army. The class members were to bring brown bag lunches, which would be eaten, picnic style at a park pavilion reserved for the occasion.

In anticipation of this outing the girls were looking through the Sears-Roebuck catalog at the latest fashions for young ladies. Their eyes lit on an outfit described as a play suit. Since refined young southern women would never dare to wear pants at that time, which was actually considered to be sinful in our part of the country, this play suit was quite daring. Not really pants, but not a skirt either it might be described as being a forerunner of culottes, which were women's knee length trousers, cut with very full legs to resemble a skirt.

They ran to Mama and showed her the picture of the play suit, begging her to let them order them. After all they had saved the few coins they had earned by dropping tobacco plants for a neighbor and could pay for the outfits themselves. Mama looked at the pictures and made her standard response, "Go ask your Daddy". Why she always said that we never knew as she always was the one to have the last word. Iva was elected to be the one to "go ask Daddy", and to make it sound more innocuous it was decided she would tell him it was just a divided skirt. Whoever made the final decision, it was ended with the play suits being ordered.

When the package came the garments were inspected and found to be beautiful by the sisters, but worrisome to Mama who felt that her permission in ordering them might lead to the wearing of slacks, which then might be worn to a shameful movie theater, or might lead to such sinful activities as playing cards or playing bingo or on to a steady decline into the gambling abyss.

In preparation for the field trip Rebecca and Iva Nel decided to press the wrinkles from their play suits, so they placed the flat iron on top of the hot cook stove to heat. Instead of getting out the rickety old ironing board they folded up a quilt on the floor and did the ironing there.

I was 3 years old, full of energy, excited because my sisters were going to get to wear divided skirts, bouncing around, tripped and fell against the very hot iron, which was sitting upright. It left the print of the iron on my leg, which became a huge blister, surrounded by large red painful areas. I was screaming in agony. Mama rushed into the room, quickly assessed what had happened, grabbed me in her arms, and ran all the way to our neighbor, Mrs. Neva Taylor's house, about one fourth mile away, with me crying loudly all the way. Everyone knew "Miss Neva" could blow fire out of a burn.

She gladly received me, and told Mama to stay in the living room. She took me into another room and closed the door. Her quiet demeanor calmed me down somewhat. I listened as she started chanting in a sing-song voice. I am not sure what she was saying but I believe she was quoting some scripture verses. She waved her hands over me, and then she began to blow on my wound. It felt so cool like a nice summer breeze. I looked at my leg. The blister had vanished. The redness was gone, as was the pain. No scar was left. Indeed there was no evidence that a burn had ever occurred. Though I was only 3 years old, and didn't understand all of the goings on, I still remember the actual occurrence vividly.

She said her gift was from the Lord and must be kept a secret, but she could pass the gift on to one non-relative, opposite-gender person. She said she would one day pass the gift to my father, but she never did, so I suppose the gift died with her.

CHAPTER 14: THE TURNIP GREENS PATCH

———◆———

"Happy is the bride that the sun shines on", Poplin thought to herself as she sprang out of bed. "And the sun is shining today and I will be a bride. And I'm already happy. So happy."

Her Mama was going to take her eggs and a pail of cream to Harris Grove to trade for groceries at the General Store, and as soon as she was out the door, Poplin pulled out the long box that had been so carefully hidden under her bed. From it she took the beautiful white dress she had ordered from the Sears Roebuck catalog. Though the dress had cost $2.95, a rather large sum to pay, the shipping was free and she was able to pay for it with the money she had earned from picking strawberries. She had been paid only 1 ½ cents for each quart she picked, but this menial chore was one of the very few opportunities a young girl in her community could earn a little pocket money. She had been successful in watching for the mail man and accepting the box without anyone seeing the transaction. Even Thomas didn't know she had the dress.

She thought of Thomas. He was ten years older than her, and had recently inherited his father's farm just up the road from her own house, moving there from up north somewhere. She reflected on the first time she had met him at his strawberry field. She remembered how he had smiled at her and seemed to spend more time with her than with the other pickers. "Oh that smile", she thought. "And those beautiful blue eyes". Then there was that first time when he put his arm around her. She had pulled away. She had been so shy. Now thinking of him she remembered his first kiss.

And finally there was the time when she stayed after the other workers had gone home, and he had gently led her into the nearby barn. Now, she could almost smell the sweet fragrance of the hay that had served as a place to lie down, when their love had been consummated.

She took the dress from the tissue paper and tried it on again. Only two weeks since it had arrived and she could already tell that it was tighter across her middle. "It's a good thing my wedding is today, as we won't be able to hide the fact that I'm expecting much longer. Poplin had heard older women relate stories about childbearing, and one such story was that a "seven month baby" would be more likely to live than an "eight month baby". This theory was built on the belief that all babies tried to kick their way out of the womb at seven months. If they were successful, with special care they might do well. But if not able to get out at seven months and if they tried again at eight months, they were so weakened by the earlier attempt that they usually succumbed. So she would marry Thomas and then let people think she had a seven month baby.

When she told Thomas about it earlier, he was upset, and certainly not happy as she thought he would be. He even suggested she visit old Mary Howe, who lived in a shack in the next county. She was known to assist in birthing babies, and was thought, perhaps, to bring about miscarriages by using certain herbs, at times. Poplin was surprised at his suggestion, but then he seemed to accept the situation. She told him that they should hurry and get married before anyone suspected the reason for the rush. He seemed preoccupied but agreed to her plan for a hasty wedding. He cautioned her not to tell anyone of their plan, not even her mother. She agreed and was looking forward to surprising everyone, especially her mother.

It was a fad at that time in the community for the bridal couple to ride in a buggy to get married under the big oak tree near Oak Grove Baptist Church. The Justice of the Peace would perform the simple ceremony and the bride and groom would not even have to get out of the buggy. So this was the plan and he was to pick her up in his buggy this afternoon. Wouldn't Mama be surprised when she would tell her she was married this very day! Perhaps the neighbors would gossip, but she would be Mrs. Thomas Mills. She loved the sound of it. Knowing that he would soon be her husband made her heart flutter. She knew she loved him and would make him proud to have her as his wife.

Poplin kept looking at the big Seth Thomas clock on the fireplace mantle. In less than an hour he would be here to pick her up. Again she looked at herself in the mirror. She smoothed her hair. Her face was flushed with excitement, so it wasn't necessary to pinch her cheeks, as she sometimes did to bring about a becoming blush. Soon she heard the sound of horse hoofs approaching. She opened the front door and looked down the gravel road, expecting to see the handsome horse and nearly new buggy belonging to Thomas. Instead it was Mama.

When Mama came in she placed her cardboard box of groceries on the kitchen table. "Baking powder has gone up to three cents," she complained. Then she saw Poplin in her new dress. "Where did you get that dress?' she asked.

"It's to wear to a wedding."

"Oh, did they invite you to their wedding, Poplin? How did you know they were getting married? Everybody at the store thought it was a hurried up case".

"What do you mean, Mama? Who got married?"

"Why Thomas Mills and Ann McReynolds. They were married this morning. Didn't you say you went to the wedding? If you can call it a wedding. Just driving up in a buggy for the Justice of the Peace to say a few words."

Poplin felt faint. She was overwhelmed with the realization that Thomas had married another woman to keep from marrying her. Here in the year 1896, to have a child out of wedlock was an unimaginable disgrace. Any hope for a future marriage was unfathomable. No man would have her now. She was damaged goods. How was she going to tell Mama? No one would consider that Thomas had duped her, but rather that she must have seduced him. That was the way that situations like this were viewed.

First there was the shame and humiliation. This was soon replaced with raging anger. As her belly grew so did a fierce desire to retaliate. But how? What could she do? She often had to hear what a good wife the new bride was. What a wonderful cook. A skilled gardener.

One night, unable to sleep, Poplin went outside. The moon was full and gave amazing light. She walked along the lane and found herself heading toward the couple's house. As she neared the house she came upon their turnip greens patch. Suddenly she knew what she had to do. Her bladder, feeling pressure from the growing baby, cooperated as she squatted and urinated over a large area of the turnip greens. A short time later she was able to repeat the act.

She experienced a small sense of satisfaction when she heard that Mrs. Mills was bragging about her expertise in growing a bountiful turnip greens patch. "Thomas just loves a salad made from the fresh turnip greens I have raised. And they are just so nice and clean. I can make his salad without even washing them first".

Poplin went to bed that night, and for the first time in many weeks went to sleep with a smile on her face.

CHAPTER 15: ZODIAC MAN

—————◆—————

Mama considered The Old Farmer's Almanac to be the Gospel when planning her garden. The almanac showed the Man of the Signs, or sometimes called The Zodiac Man, which was a drawing of a man whose body parts corresponded to the 12 signs of the zodiac. She knew exactly when to plant certain vegetables. For example root vegetables that grow in the ground, such as carrots, potatoes, onions, beets should be planted when the "signs are in the feet", which would be Pisces. Sweet peas should not be planted later than the last part of the Aquarius sign, February, as they can tolerate very cold even freezing weather if their stems have less that three knuckles, but will not do well if weather gets very hot. Vegetables that grow well above the ground, for example corn, should be planted when the signs are in the head and face, Aries. When seeds were planted according to this strict schedule the weather always seemed to cooperate and the temperature and rainfall would be ideal, leading to a bountiful harvest.

The Farmer's Almanac proposes that when the moon is in the correct place in the zodiac, certain activities will be more fruitful and lead to improved results.

Many of our neighbors relied on the almanac to choose the best times to set hens to get the most eggs to hatch; the best time to wean a baby, to potty train a child; or even when to try to schedule a pregnancy so the baby would be born at an opportune time.

Some believed in consulting the Zodiac Man for choosing the best time to quit smoking or maybe when to have wisdom teeth pulled.

Along the same lines, we were always keeping count of how many foggy mornings we had in the month of August, for we would then expect to have that many snow falls the following winter. Other time- honored signs of a harsh winter that we noted were when the wild, honking geese headed south early in the season, and the squirrels started gathering nuts furiously. Then when the "wooly worms" seemed to have an extra thick fur-like coat, we assumed that was because they would need the extra fur as the winter was going to be very cold.

We kids admired Mama's knowledge and expertise which she demonstrated in such an interesting, as well as tried-and-true, ways.

CHAPTER 16: SHOUTING
IN CHURCH

————◆————

Members of Sinking Spring Southern Missionary Baptist Church were very faithful in their attendance at services year round. Of course in the late 1930's there was no air conditioning. So in the hot summer time the women cooled themselves with the little cardboard fans distributed by a local funeral home. On one side of the fan was a beautiful full color picture of Jesus, sitting on a big stone, surrounded by little children. Across the top of the picture in large letters was the Bible verse, "Suffer the little children to come unto me. Matthew 19: 14". On the other side was an advertisement, in equally large letters, from the J. H. Churchill Funeral Home, the benefactor of the fans. It included the image of their earliest conveyance, a horse drawn hearse. As Mama fanned me I was wondering why the children in the picture were suffering when they had such big smiles on their faces.

The women always wore hats and dresses, and would never be seen in pants. The men wore suits and ties, and fedora hats. I was so fascinated with the tiny little feather in the band around Papa's hat.

It was believed that women should not speak up in church. This was based on the scripture found in I Corinthians 14:34 "Let your women keep silence in the churches: for it is not permitted unto them to speak...." So all decisions and actions regarding the church were left to the men, or so it was thought. In reality everyone knew the men were just following the instructions their wives had given them.

Often the sermons were long, and though there was a small nursery adjacent to the sanctuary, it was only for babies. Children of toddler age or older were expected to sit still beside their parents. If a child misbehaved or disturbed the congregation, a parent would take the child outside for a "correction". Upon returning to the service the child would be quiet.

Mrs. Jones would always sit in a chair in the nursery-sanctuary doorway and breast feed her baby during services. She was ahead of her day as she didn't wean the infants until they were at least two years old. And she seemed to always have a baby! She would get very emotionally involved with the sermon, and ironically, given the prohibition of women speaking in church, she would begin "Holy ghost shouting", which may be defined as being filled with the spirit and overjoyed with blessings from the Lord. She would cry out loudly, "Praise the Lord. Amen. Hallelujah! " And then some other unintelligible words. I wasn't sure what was happening, but I wondered if perhaps the nursing baby had bit her.

CHAPTER 17: THE AUTHORESS

———•———

I was a "change of life" baby, a term used to describe babies born to women approaching menopause. In fact I was born on my father's 41st birthday and Mama was one year younger. Since I was the youngest of five children, my two older sisters doted on me. Perhaps getting to baby sit the new sibling instead of going to the field to work may have been some of the allure. Hugh Thomas, my brother who was three years older than me, was not so thrilled to be preempted from his status as youngest child. Upon seeing me for the first time, and failing to see anything as wonderful as the older kids seemed to see, he voiced his assessment by commenting, "Her head looks just like a coconut!"

Since my sisters were privileged seniors when I entered first grade, they usually waited for the late bus by spending the time in the Principal's office. They couldn't understand why I would rather play outside in the cold weather with my friends, so they would occasionally coax me to come inside the office where it was warm. Upon entering the office I noticed the large letters OFFICE etched on the glass in the top portion of the door. Being very astute, I concluded that meant the room was warm,,,hence OFF ICE.

I had mastered the Dick and Jane book early on and was an avid reader. It seemed logical that I would also want to be a writer. And so it was, even as a child, my latent writing ability was straining to break forth, but it wasn't until a few years later that the post-war baby boom gave me the first vehicle to develop those creative talents. I had read about Brenda Starr, Girl Reporter, and I could hardly wait to follow in her foot steps. I had searched our weekly newspaper for ideas, and had envisioned eventually having a syndicated column of my own. Finally I decided on a suitable undertaking. It would be a beginning to an illustrious career! I wrote my literary contribution, read it, and revised it many times. Finally it was perfect. With real pride I submitted my masterpiece by mail, anonymously, to our local paper, *The Ledger and Times.*

I eagerly awaited the mailman that next Friday, and relieved him of the newspaper without the necessity of placing it in the mailbox. Mama noticed my marked interest in the newspaper, but I was careful that she didn't see I was passing over the comics, and turning instead to the Birth Announcements.

There it was! I'll never forget the thrill when I saw my own creation in print. With great pride I read my already familiar prose: Mr. and Mrs. James Brown announce the birth of a son, George Albert, on Tuesday, April 8. Weight 7 pounds 11 ounces. Grand parents are Mr. and Mrs. Carl Brown and Mr. and Mrs. Ben Colley. I closed my eyes. It was poetic. I placed myself in the same league with another great writer of birth announcements: "...and Abraham begat Isaac, and Isaac begat...." And even the celestial announcements "...for unto you this day is born...."

No one could have been prouder. But Mama never scolded me for submitting that fictitious birth announcement and I was never punished. That's because I never told anyone—until now.

CHAPTER 18: NON-SUPERSTITIOUS SUPERSTITIONS

———◆———

Mrs. Alma Belle Phillips would be the first to deny the validity of superstitions. "Why superstitions are of the devil. They're witchcraft. That's what they are, just like fortune telling," she said. "And being a Christian I would not want to be associated with that kind of evil. But I know that some of those old sayings aren't superstitions. Some folks may just call them 'old wives' tales' but there's a lot of truth in some of them. "

One of those "facts" she was referring to was "Never do your laundry on New Year's Day, because if you do you'll lose your husband before the year is over." And as proof of the verity of this old adage she described what happened with her neighbor. "Why Jane Crider's husband had a stroke six years ago, and though he was confined to his bed and it took two people to get him up in a wheel chair, he *was* living. She had never washed laundry on this auspicious day before and her husband had always survived the year. Then last year she said she just had to wash his bed clothes on New Year's Day, as he was incontinent and everything was wet and smelly. Now Jane knew not to wash clothes on that day but she decided there was nothing to that notion so she went ahead and washed the sheets. And sure enough on May 27 of that same year her husband died. So there you are. You see, that wasn't a superstition. That was a fact. She said she would just have to live with it."

It is not known if this was a gender-specific belief, applying only to women losing their husbands if they broke that rule. And we'll never know, for no where in that vicinity in that age had there ever been a man who did any laundry—on New Year's Day, or any other day.

Other beliefs associated with New Year's Day were widely practiced in the neighborhood. Everyone should get up early and work hard all day, as this meant you would have a job all year. But manage to take time out to visit a neighbor (this would mean there'd be friends all year) and be sure to take a gift of food, especially a jar of jam, or a jar of homemade pickles made from a special recipe that had been in the family for generations, to assure the family would be blessed with a full larder in the coming months. Then await the mandatory reciprocal visit from friends, such as Dennis and Maggie Boyd, coming to visit, with food items in hand. Later when the visitor's jam was served, the whole family declared Mama's to be far superior. Black eyed peas cooked with hog's jowl straight from the smoke house, would be served at dinner and possibly also at supper, just for good measure, to make doubly sure good luck would bless the future. All the businesses that catered to farmers gave free calendars to their customers around Christmas time. Hanging the new calendars on New Year's Day was quite a ritual and everyone knew it was bad luck to hang them even one day early.

But Mrs. Phillips was not through talking about her non-superstitious superstitions. Fridays were generally considered bad luck, like Friday the 13th. Some say this connotation was because Christ was crucified on a Friday. "Mama always said that if you trimmed your fingernails on Friday you'd be disappointed. She was never specific about what the disappointment would be. But she really believed it. Now I don't think there's anything to it but if I have a hangnail on Friday morning, well it can just wait until Saturday. After all, there's no harm in making sure, just in case".

Her mama was also given credit for believing in some lore having to do with the hands. If the palm of the left hand itches it means you are going to receive money. But if the right palm itches you are going to shake hands with a stranger, Mrs. Phillips claimed to have no faith in this belief either.

"But", she added, "if my right palm itches enough so that I find myself scratching it, I'm going to get up and straighten up the place. I don't want anyone, let alone strangers, think I'm a sloppy housekeeper."

If she accidently dropped her dish cloth on the floor she'd say, "Well someone's coming who's a worse house keeper than I am". She even had little rhymes that accompanied some of her sayings, like "My nose itches. Someone's coming with a hole in her britches".

My own mother, affectionately known as Mama Jewel by everyone in the neighborhood, loved to have all the food eaten that she had prepared. She would encourage the family to scrape the bowls, because this would assure that tomorrow would be a fair day. And she could forecast the weather, quite accurately I might add, by listening to how loud she could hear the evening train whistle from Murray. If the sound was especially loud then she would predict "falling weather".

Our elderly neighbor, Mr. Leonard Paschall, would never get a haircut in the month of March, thus preventing the possibility of having headaches .And the Cathcarts who were share croppers in the Taylor Store community would not allow any evergreens to grow in their yard. A pine seedling came up, probably dropped by a passing bird, and as soon as it was seen, Mrs. Cathcart had it dug up and destroyed. She was quick to inform others about the danger of evergreens, giving this advice: "Never let an evergreen tree grow on your land because as soon as it grows tall enough to shade your grave you will surely die".

CHAPTER 19: COUSIN BOBBIE

Cousin Bobbie was an itinerant traveling piano teacher. She would come spend some time in peoples' homes and teach piano lessons to the children in exchange for room and board, plus a small fee. Cousin Bobbie was a sprightly older woman, with a gentle demeanor, and quick smile, who was actually nobody's cousin.

It was our turn to host Cousin Bobbie, and though we didn't have a piano we did have an ancient organ. Rebecca and Iva Nel were the only children at our house who were old enough to take music lessons. Iva Nel was thrilled and eager to learn. Rebecca detested the sessions and said the only thing worse was de-worming the fields of tobacco, where the big fat green worms were manually pulled from the plants and thoroughly mashed, so that their tobacco chewing days were no more.

When it was Rebecca's turn to practice at the organ she feigned a terrible headache. She gained a lot of sympathy from gullible Cousin Bobbie, who responded by putting Rebecca in a rocking chair propped up with many pillows, swathing her brow with cool wet wash cloths, and she then pulled all the window shades down thinking a darkened room would be soothing. She even decided she would play some soft organ music that might help Rebecca relax, and possibly inspire her to practice when her head ache was relieved. Alas, while she was pumping the pedal on the organ the belt that held it in place broke! The purpose of the pedal was to pump air which generated sound as the air passed through a vibrating piece of metal called a reed. Without a functioning pedal the organ was inoperable.

Rebecca's headache miraculously disappeared and she went skipping happily down to the hen house where Iva Nel was gathering the eggs. "The organ pedal is broken! The organ pedal is broken! No more music lessons", she reported.

But Cousin Bobbie's resources were sorely underestimated. To quote an old adage, "Where there is a will there's a way". She went to the horse barn, found a good harness strap Papa used on his mules, cut it up and made a replacement binder belt for the organ pedal.

The music lessons resumed. So did the headaches.

But the plowing could not resume until Papa could purchase another harness strap for his mule.

CHAPTER 20: STRAW HAT DAY

——————

Friday was Peddler Day. One of the kids would be on the look out for the big truck. Some still called it a peddling wagon, a phrase left over from the times when the merchandise was actually brought on a wagon pulled by two horses. In the olden days that was by necessity in the winter times when the roads were in such bad shape that motor vehicles would have mired down.

On this day the peddler would just pull the truck over and park by the side of the gravel road in front of our house. No need to worry about interfering with the flow of traffic. Passing cars were few and far between. It was like a small country store, except it came to us. There were grocery staples, school supplies, candy bars that caught the children's eyes, and in the spring even straw hats. That's where the family members would get their mandatory annual straw hats to be worn for protection from the sun while working in the fields.

So when the peddler came we all went out. There was much ado about selecting the new straw hats from the littlest to the oldest. My brother, Lynn was just a little boy at this yearly ritual. One of the older kids picked up the largest adult size hat and just for fun put it on Lynn's head. It was so large that he could turn his head around without the hat moving. Mimicking what he had heard adults say when completing a purchase, he said, "I believe I'll take it".

CHAPTER 21: THE GREAT DEPRESSION

When people lived through the Great Depression, which lasted from 1929 through 1939, their lives were changed forever. Though most of it was over before my time I have heard my parents speak of the terrible hardships endured. My family was fortunate to be able to raise most of their food, vegetable gardens and "truck patches", chickens for eggs and meat, a cow for milk and butter, and several hogs to be butchered in the cold winter time to provide fresh meat as well as cured meat that could be kept all year. Wheat was grown to be ground into flour, from which Mama made her delicious biscuits; same for the corn that would be ground into meal for our staple, cornbread.

But there were many families nearby who were less fortunate. One morning when Mama went into the smoke house to cut some slices from the country ham hanging there, the ham was gone! The sacks of wheat and corn were kept in the hay loft in the barn. Then it was discovered that most of the sacks of grain had been stolen too. Papa said it wasn't because people were dishonest or mean; they were just hungry.

During this time the summer week of revival at our church was still being held. In fact it seemed that in such troubled times attendance was increased. The visiting evangelist conducted a service in the afternoon and another at night. These services were of such high importance that farmers took time out from their work to attend both sessions. Mama and the two older girls had very few clothes so they would wash one set of clothes in the morning and hang them on the line to dry, so they would have fresh clothes to wear that night. One day when they came home from the afternoon service—lo and behold!—someone had stolen all their clothes from the line.

Banks had failed early on, and Papa lost what money he had in it. But he happened to still have his money he had received as a bonus for his military service in the Great War, so he was able to pay his property taxes and save our farm from foreclosure. He was even able to loan a neighbor, Mr. Gary Myers, money to pay his taxes too. Another farm saved!

I heard them reminisce about the hardships of those times, but I was young and didn't pay much attention. After it was too late I wished I had written it down.

CHAPTER 22: ELECTRICITY COMES TO WISWELL

Papa had just had our house wired for electricity in 1941, but before all the connecting wires could be placed, the outbreak of war called a halt to such enterprises, and it would be years before electricity would arrive at the Wilkerson household. Most of our light fixtures consisted of a single bulb in the ceiling with a pull chain hanging down. As the kids would run through the house we would reach up and pull a chain, pretending to have lights. When we were finally connected to power some of the lights had been left in the on-position, and we screamed with delight when light flooded the room. But some of them had been left in the off-position, and when there was no light immediately from them we feared they were defective, until we realized the remedy was to pull the chains again.

At the beginning of WWII we were one of just a few families in the community who had a radio, and it was battery operated and batteries were soon on the list of items rationed, so usage was limited. But in the evening after all the chores were done we were all allowed to listen to the popular show, "Jack Armstrong, the All American Boy". And when the William Tell Overture announced the "Lone Ranger" show, adults, as well as the children hovered around the radio to hear the saga of the mysterious cowboy, and his side-kick, Tonto, who together rousted out the villains, proving that good could once again overcome evil. It was such a thrill to hear the cowboy shout," Hi Yo, Silver", as he rode away with the sound of the hoof beats fading away into the airways, Then a voice would always say, "Who was that masked man?" He always left a silver bullet as his calling card but his identity was never known. But we felt very privileged that we had been let in on the secret; we knew it was the Lone Ranger!

Occasionally we listened to "The Stella Dallas" show, an early version of a daytime soap opera, which was indeed sponsored by a soap, Duz laundry detergent. Mama still preferred her homemade lye soap, even though the Duz manufacturer enticed buyers by placing a piece of glassware, or even a dinner plate in each box. Their slogan was "Duz does everything", which we thought was a clever jingle. It didn't take much to entertain us.

On Saturday nights several of our neighbors would bring their children and come to our house. They would sit around the radio and listen to "The Grand Ole Opry" broadcast from Nashville, Tennessee, while all the children were outside playing Hide-and-Seek, and catching lightning bugs and putting them into Mason jars.

It would be several years before television would make its impact on our community. Mrs. Grace Clark was the first to own one, a black and white picture set. Again neighbors would congregate at her house to watch the wildly popular "I Love Lucy" show, which would generate enough discussion to last until the next week's episode.

Such neighborly occasions represented a welcome break in the arduous back-breaking work of everyday farm life.

CHAPTER 23: OUR TELEPHONE

O ur radio was our most valued source of entertainment, but our telephone was a close second. Ours was a nice wooden box made of oak. There was a bell on top, that made the ringing sound, the receiver hung on the left side, and on the right was the ringer, a little handle that turned. It was attached to the wall in the kitchen, the room most likely to be occupied. A stool stood nearby to be used by the younger kids, to elevate them to be able to speak into the mouth piece.

The main switchboard was in Harris Grove, and there were several party lines. Our line was number 25, and there were several households on our line. Each of us were assigned a certain number of rings; ours were two longs, meaning if someone on our own line wanted to talk to us they would simply turn the ringer two long rings, which would ring in our telephone. It would also ring in everyone else's phone on our line. Other numbers were something like two shorts, or one long and two shorts, etc. If we wanted to talk to someone on another line we had to go through Central. The switchboard lady was Mrs. Rema Cole, who took her job so seriously that she was known to break into a conversation and make corrections to some of the information being transmitted. Or if she believed someone was hogging the lines she just might decide not to put through a few of their calls. Woe to the young suitor who might try to call his girlfriend if Mrs. Cole thought the match unsuitable.

So if anyone on Line 25 received a call it would ring in everybody's phone, and it was considered the duty of all subscribers to listen in. But not just listen, but perhaps join in on the conversation, especially if they had more current news that could be added. So no one thought this unusual or an infringement on one's privacy, because everyone did the same thing.

CHAPTER 24: PAPA'S SHOES

On this cold wintery Saturday night the fire in the living room fireplace was blazing. Earlier that day my older brother had convinced me that Santa used the sparks from the burning logs to make dolls. So I had dutifully used the poker to make an abundance of sparks go up the chimney on their way to the North Pole.

When I grew tired of sending Santa material for dolls I noticed Papa's shoes setting near the hearth, all polished and shiny, ready for wearing to church the next morning. I thought what fun it would be to wear them, so I put my feet into those size 12 shoes, so heavy I could barely lift my feet in them, and went clomping around the room.

Even though I was just a small child I was very inquisitive. I pestered my family with questions about everything under the sun. I heard grown-ups say, admiringly, that I had a vivid imagination and a keen sense of curiosity. Then I began to wonder. What would happen if I kicked the shoes into the fireplace? Would they burn? Or would they survive just like Daniel in the fiery furnace? I didn't know about the research process or terminology at this tender age, but I did know that to test the hypothesis I would need to carry out the experiment. So I kicked one shoe into the fire, but the sudden realization of possible consequences occurred to me, so I didn't follow through with the second shoe.

Perhaps it was the smell of burning leather that alerted Mama, and she ran into the room and with the poker pulled the charred remnant of the shoe from the fire. The shoe was beyond recognition, and the fact that it was just one shoe sacrificed to research seemed to be of no consolation to her. Knowing that I was somehow in danger of a good scolding or maybe worse, I crawled under the bed. Thinking in terms of a three year old, I hoped that if I was not seen perhaps the deed would be undone.

I heard Mama and Papa discussing the matter, trying to decide if I was old enough to be aware of the seriousness of my offence, and if so, what kind of punishment would be fitting. They relied on the Biblical writings as a child-rearing manual, most specifically the "Spare the rod and spoil the child" admonition. Mama dragged me, unwillingly, from underneath the bed, and I received my first (of many to come) spanking.

It was too late to go to town and buy more shoes, and since this was his only pair of Sunday shoes, Papa had to forego church that Sunday morning, which prevented him from receiving the coveted pin for perfect attendance for 25 years.

CHAPTER 25: UNCLE CRATIC

—————•—————

He was a kind and gentle man, my Uncle Cratic. He had a quiet and retiring personality, and seemed to be perpetually smiling. I would call him the epitome of a good man, the kind of man who no one ever spoke ill of. And I never heard him speak unkindly of any person. Born in the late 1880's, he was a product of his times. He believed in hard work and self sufficiency. When government subsidies to over-worked under-paid farmers were initiated he refused the offer as he felt he had not earned it. Then in his later years, though he paid his taxes as soon as they came due, at age 65 he refused to apply for social security. He was too proud to ask for help from anyone, financial or otherwise. Yet he was quick to assist anyone in need

He was married to my Aunt Lizzie, and together they were life partners, living on their farm. Actually he was very dependent on her. She laughingly once said, "If he needs to nail up a board I would need to be there to hand him the hammer". They never had children, but Aunt Lizzie adored her sister, Margie, who was several years younger. And they also had a special place in their hearts for their nephews and nieces; I was the youngest. A little neighbor boy, Carl, could frequently be found at their house, to their delight. We all loved to spend time with Uncle Cratic and Aunt Lizzie. And we loved the watermelons they grew. They were certainly champion watermelon growers, and the melons were huge. They once brought a big watermelon to our house and it was too heavy to weigh on our farm scales so we had to cut it into two pieces and weigh each piece separately.

Sometimes Aunt Lizzie would decide to make a dress for me. She had a yardstick for measuring fabric, but she thought that was too new fangled to use and instead measured the cloth by holding it up and stretching it from the tip of her nose to the thumb of her outstretched hand, and then declaring it an exact yard of material. All scraps of left over fabric would be saved for making quilt pieces, which were pieced together and then quilted by hand. It was fun later, as we nestled under the covers, to identify which pieces of the quilt had been from whose dress.

Though Uncle Cratic and Aunt Lizzie complemented each other, their roles were sharply delineated according to gender. I'm certain he never cooked a bite of food nor washed a dish, but he was viewed as the head of the house.

Guests were always welcome in their house where delicious southern home cooked meals were served. Prior to coming to the table everyone was asked to wash their face and hands in the communal wash basin and a cloth feed sack, soft from repeated launderings, served as a towel. Beside the wash basin was the old oaken water bucket, which was holding cold water fresh from a spring, not drawn from a well. In the bucket was a communal dipper, homemade from a gourd. Everyone drank straight from the dipper. A new dipper was made each fall, from his home grown gourds, which had been carved to resemble a ladle, the seeds removed, and then it was dried in the sun.

At the dinner table Uncle Cratic would always ask the male guest to "return thanks", though I never heard him say the blessing himself. A pone of cornbread baked in a cast iron skillet always accompanied the dinner and supper meals. The cornbread was never sliced before serving; instead it was placed on a plate and passed around the table with each person breaking off a piece, because he thought this was Biblical: "the breaking of the bread".

It was also an admonition from the Bible that caused Aunt Lizzie to never cut her hair. Rather she would fashion it into a very long beautiful braid and coil it around her head and fasten it with a tortoise shell comb, a wedding gift from Uncle Cratic. And so her sister, Margie now considered an "old maid", did not cut her own hair either.

As a young man, Uncle Cratic bought a Model A Ford, which had to be started by inserting a crank in the front and turning it until the motor fired off. He just started driving it without any instructions. As time went on he would trade for newer models. When I was about two or three years old my parents and I were riding in his latest vehicle when he had an accident. I'm not sure what he hit. It's doubtful it was another car as there were so few around. My head hit the top of the car and I was taken to a hospital to be checked. Though I was only a toddler I can still remember seeing the doctor with a strange looking reflector light on his forehead. And if I really try I can still remember that new car smell.

He didn't like nicknames or shortened versions of words, and if faced with an abbreviations, might just complete the term as he saw appropriate. For example when he was reading the weekly newspaper, he noted, "It says here that a lot of people in New York City don't even own cars. Instead they just hail one of them yellow tax-i cabinets."

Though Uncle Cratic lived to be an old man, and he had many cars, he apparently never had any driving instructions. His neighbor, Carl (the little boy, grown up) still remembers how Uncle Cratic would slip the clutch and race the engine, while trying to shift gears, grinding away while blue smoke came from the exhaust. And he would never go more than 25 miles an hour. Aunt Lizzie never tried to learn to drive their car, though Margie did sometimes drive.

It was a sad day when we heard that Aunt Lizzie had terminal cancer. She received loving care from her family and neighbors, and toward the end Uncle Cratic didn't leave her bedside. A few days before she died she called my mother to come closer to her bed. She told her, "You know Cratic doesn't know how to cook or manage a house. He won't even be able to take care of himself. So I've been thinking about this for a long time," She stopped for a minute to take a deep breath. Then she went on "I've decided I want him to marry Margie. She will take care of him for me. And he'll be good to her".

At that time Margie had been considered a spinster woman for some time. After the requisite year of mourning, they were married and lived happily for several years. They had a little dog, Bounce, who they trained, on command, to jump up on the first three steps leading upstairs, where he would be rewarded for this feat by catching pieces of leftover biscuits that they tossed to him. When visitors came they were always treated to this exhibition, of which they took great pride.

Some time after Uncle Cratic died, a neighbor, Sylvia Dell, established a beauty salon in her home. She told Aunt Margie if she would let her cut her hair she would give her a free perm. So the haircut and perm procedure was accomplished. And I believe that she received free hair styling for the rest of her life.

Then Aunt Margie moved to a little house in town. She quickly became acclimated to her new neighborhood, and made lots of friends. And she obtained her most prized possession-- a black dial-up telephone. The city phone was also a party line and her favorite pastime was talking or listening in on the phone. We said she suffered from the "black cord syndrome". She bought a nice used car, and she would drive down her street, with the clutch slipping, a grinding noise accompanying the gear shift, and blue smoke coming out the exhaust, and always at 25 miles per hour. It was easy to guess who had taught her to drive.

Now Uncle Cratic lies in the Sinking Spring Baptist Church cemetery, and Aunt Lizzie is buried next to him on his left, and Aunt Margie is buried on his right,

May they rest in peace.